Tax Problems? Paying Too Much? Afraid of Audits?

Tax Strategies for Real Estate Professionals

Published by CordaNobelo

Edition 1st

ISBN 978-0-9857719-6-6

Dedicated to:
Lydia Guzman, MPH, RD
Glen & Margie Thompson
Jose & Consuelo Rodriguez

"If Patrick Henry though that taxation without representation was bad, he should see how bad it is with representation."

Farmer's Almanac

"I contend that for a nation to try to tax itself into prosperity is like a man standing in a bucket and trying to lift himself up by the handle."

Winston Churchill

Contents

How to Get Maximum Value from this Book

You've heard that knowledge is power! This is only half-true. In reality, power comes from the use of knowledge, not the mere possession of it.

You can get the most from this book by taking the ideas and concepts in this book that apply to you and putting them into action, putting them to use.

How do you put this knowledge into use?

Paying too much in taxes?

If you feel like you *pay WAY TOO MUCH in TAXES*, you are not alone! In fact, the Government Accountability Office estimates that taxpayers overpay taxes by about $945 million each year due to mistakes they and their tax preparers make on their tax returns! Not surprising because the tax system is getting more and more complicated. You may want to move forward by implementing my recommendations on your own, or you may benefit from professional assistance. Because you have purchased this book and are actively searching for ways to reduce your taxes, I'm offering my services to help you develop and implement your tax saving plan at a reduced rate. I'm making this offer because after reading this book you will be better informed and my job will be easier.

I wrote this book, to empower you! But, I am also here to help you.

If working with a professional to *ProActively* save taxes and protect yourself from tax audits works best for you, I would be happy to talk with you about our *Tax Coaching* Program.

Contact me within 30 days of purchasing this book and you will get 20% off your Tax Coaching Program. Just send me an e-mail (fred@fthompsoncpa.com) with your purchase receipt and contact information. Write "Offer #501" in the subject line. I will contact you to discuss your situation to see if you can benefit from our *ProActive Tax Coaching* Program.

Oh, and by the way, don't let physical distance stop you. I work with people all over the United States and internationally using the latest communication and computer tools.

Overview of our *ProActive* Tax Strategy Program

The goal of *ProActive Tax Coaching* is to help you keep more of what you earn by using legal tax deductions and loopholes that allow you to take control of your taxes!

There are two stages to the *ProActive Tax Coaching* Program:

(1) Start with a *ProActive* Tax Strategy that looks at each aspect of your business and investments as they pertain to tax strategies and asset protection, and

(2) Continue saving as your wealth grows with ongoing Tax Coaching.

Benefit to you

You are making an investment. Like any other investment, you must get a return on your money! The benefits you'll get from a *ProActive* Strategy will come to you in many ways:

- Save taxes
- Audit protection
- Protect assets
- Enhanced wealth building capabilities
- Peace of mind from knowing that you have an expert financial team that supports you so you can concentrate on what you do best
- Accountability - we stand behind what we deliver

Our clients save thousands in tax by with our *ProActive* Tax Strategies.

I am a small business owner with large enterprise background and experience and with the unbashful intention of making money and holding on to it. Bring in the cavalry by working with Frederick Thompson, CPA, CTC. Fred thrives on finding solutions that work and suggests tailored and personalized approaches. He is able to translate financial information as well as tax rules and reporting requirements from Gibberish into plain English. Fred loves to find alternative ways to save tax; he wants to understand your business and he acts as your confidant and sounding board every day, every month. With lots of hands-on experience, his is active in several professional societies. Fred has proven to be resourceful, and relentless in seeking answers and solutions. He has saved us a bucket full of dollars every year for the last five years and we are planning to do some more this year.

Harry Roussard, Foster City

I have worked with Fred for the past twenty years personally and also with him serving as an expert for clients involved in disputes concerning real estate and businesses. Fred is efficient and cordial to work with. I frequently seek out Fred's advice about tax reduction strategies, especially for real estate.

Wayne A. McFadden, Esq., San Mateo

Preface

My father worked long hours six days a week in his business manufacturing lighting fixtures. Only after he died did I learn how much he struggled to make ends meet. From the age of twelve, I was working in the business on Saturdays and summers. I can't say that I was always happy with this situation, but the experience gave me an appreciation for and an understanding of business. When I escaped and went to college, I decided that I wanted to become a Certified Public Accountant. After college, I went to work for a CPA firm doing financial audits to get the required experience, passed the CPA exam, and received my CPA license. I enjoyed auditing because it allowed me to see many businesses on a very intimate level. However, I soon learned that most businesspersons were overwhelmed with income taxes—coping with complex rules and regulations and paying too much to the government.

I realized the great need for tax planning and strategies to empower clients to take advantage of the tax system to lower their taxes. I found that the environment in CPA firms focused more on compliance rather than helping people lower taxes. I found that most CPAs focus on recording history by preparing financial statements or filling out income tax returns. They are reactionary rather than proactive. I saw many clients who were not taking advantage of opportunities to lower their taxes. The emphasis was on preparing the tax return as quickly as possible and moving onto the next one—especially during the busy tax season. Unfortunately, my father did not benefit from my new insights.

I started my own tax and accounting practice some twenty years ago to offer something different, to *ProActively* empower clients to lower their taxes, to not pay more than is legally required, and to protect themselves from tax audits

And, I specialize in working with real estate professionals because they are usually in business. Because, people in business can benefit the most from the *ProActive* tax planning strategies that I provide!

Introduction

In 1849 California prospectors flocked to the hills to find gold. I love finding hidden treasure too; but I find it in the mistakes and missed opportunities that cost taxpayers thousands of dollars. As an example a couple of years ago I helped a real estate broker, I'll call Mr. Brown, put $55,000 in his family's bank account that otherwise would have gone to the government.

Mr. Brown approached me afraid that if he didn't do something he was going to have a major tax problem. I was a little skeptical but as we looked at his situation, I realized that yes, he was right; he was going to owe the government a lot of money. And, what was more important was that there was something we could do about it. It was late in the year so we had to move fast.

Mr. Brown had two businesses, one was organized as an S Corporation, and the other that his wife ran was organized as a limited liability company (LLC). They were both doing great and were looking at passing through several hundred thousand dollars in taxable income to Mr. Brown creating a tax obligation of some $80,000. I discovered that his prior accountant did not deduct interest Mr. Brown paid on his credit cards, thinking that it was nondeductible personal interest. I found out that Mr. Brown borrowed from the credit cards and loaned the money to his wife's business. Therefore, the interest was actually investment interest that was deductible against investment income. We amended his prior three years' income tax returns to report some $40,000 of investment interest that we carried forward to the current year. The businesses paid $40,000 in interest to Mr. Brown for the loans he had made over the years. The business got a deduction and the income paid to Mr. Brown was offset by the investment interest expense carried forward from the prior years. Bottom line, we were able to deduct in the current year the credit card interest that Mr. Brown paid; the interest that his prior accountant dismissed as being nondeductible. I also learned that both businesses did not have enough office space so Mr. Brown set-up a home office from which to manage the businesses. By complying with the tax law for the home office deduction, he was able to deduct a portion of his home expenses as legitimate businesses expenses. In addition, we made sure that Mr. Brown paid in enough tax withholding through his wages to avoid potential penalties for underpayment of tax. As is common with a lot of real estate professionals, I also discovered that Mr. Brown's son helped in his business without pay. Mr. Brown was able to pay him $15,000 that was the value of his services. Mr. Brown's son paid a small amount of tax on his wage while Mr. Brown was able to save about $7,000 from the business deduction.

While I was preparing the California LLC tax return, I was surprised to learn that the California LLC tax went from $3,300 in the prior year to $6,800. In California there is something called an annual fee based on gross receipts. In the prior year, because the business gross income was a little less than one million dollars, the annual fee was $2,500, but this year the gross income was about $1,200,000. An LLC with gross income between $1,000,000 and $5,000,000 pays an annual fee of $6,000. I could not believe my eyes. If the gross income were only one dollar over one million the annual fee would go up by $3,500. Who could have thought up such a thing! The LLC was able to elect Subchapter S tax treatment and completely avoid the annual fee. His tax went from $6,800 to $800! And there was absolutely no downside.

Therefore, Mr. Brown's tax went from $80,000 to $25,000, a saving of $55,000. The cost to do this, about $5,000. Talk about a return on investment; some 1100%. And Mr. Brown will continue to save future taxes for the home office deduction and salaries paid to his son. Also his son can use the money to pay for his summer vacations instead of Mr. Brown having to write a check. In a roundabout way, this is like deducting the cost of his son's summer vacation! What's more, Mr. Brown is still a client and I love helping him continue to save taxes.

Another story: One of three owner/employees of a corporation needed to take a disability retirement because of a heart condition. Their corporation was providing disability insurance for the three owner/employees. Any disability benefits received by the owner/employee under this arrangement would be taxable. Fortunately, before he retired on disability they consulted me. We were able to change how they handled the insurance so that the benefits paid became tax-free.

The owner/employee retired on disability, and the monthly payments that he now gets every month are tax free— putting several thousand dollars in his pocket each year that would have otherwise gone to the Internal Revenue Service and the State of California.

I love this. Finding the mistakes and missed opportunities that are costing taxpayers thousands. Who says tax accountants don't have fun?

"Fight taxes through awareness."

Fred Thompson

"For every tax problem there is solution which is straight forward, uncomplicated, *and wrong*."

Anonymous

Myths

There are several myths that cause people to pay more tax than they need to.

Myth #1: My accountant/tax preparer takes care of me. Most accountants/tax preparers are reactionary. After the end of the year, you cannot do much to lower taxes except to uncover all the tax deductions that you already have, or to put money into a retirement plan. And to put all the numbers on the forms. The real tax saving opportunities come from writing history, from taking the initiative to manage when and how you receive income and pay expenses. And choosing the best form of doing business. Tax planning starts before the tax year begins not when you are filling out the tax return.

Myth #2: There is not much you can do about taxes; all you can do is just put the numbers on the forms and write a check. The biggest mistake I see people make is FAILURE TO PLAN. The government writes tax laws to influence our behavior by reducing our tax burden if we do, or don't do certain things. There are literally thousands of things we can do to reduce our taxes and reach our goals. But, we need to take the initiative. The government has a default plan, a plan which will result in more taxes than if we take the initiative to manage our taxes in advance, before the end of the year.

Myth #3: The tax authorities know the rules. There are so many tax rules and they change each day that it is impossible for anyone to know them. There are rules, there are exceptions to the rules, and there are exceptions to the exceptions. And many times there are questions that have no answers—that is why we have courts. In addition, there are different jurisdictions that sometimes interpret rules differently. In this case, we have the Supreme Court of the United States to set uniform standards, but the Supreme Court does not take up every discrepancy. To complicate matters even further, you're dealing with a bureaucracy made up of people. The bureaucracy and each of the individuals within it has a bias to interpret things in ways that they are comfortable with.

Myth #3: Taxes are impossible to control. While taxes are difficult to understand, the key is to accept the ambiguity and move forward. The encouraging news is that you don't have to understand everything—you only have to understand the things that can help you (e.g. save you money and protect you from tax audits) and the things that can hurt you (make you pay more than you need to and subject you to penalties). This is a much more manageable task.

Myth #4: I won't get audited. Today most taxpayers are audited without even knowing it—through the automatic matching of information returns (those pesky little forms you get from your bank and broker). The IRS, using the awesome power of their computers, matches the information reported on these forms with what is reported on your income tax return. If something doesn't match, you'll get a personal letter from the IRS. While the chance of getting a personal invitation from the IRS is statistically small, it is best to protect yourself from the chance of an audit by knowing the tax rules that affect you and keeping the proper documentation.

Myth #5: The only certainty in life is Death and Taxes. While I can't dispute this about death, you can nevertheless put off death and improve the quality of the time you do have by leading a healthy lifestyle. But taxes! That is another story. I can't promise that you can always eliminate taxes, that would not be true. Many times there are legal ways to reduce taxes and sometimes completely eliminate them. Most of the time you need to take the initiative to do so!

Who this book is for

Are you in the real estate business?
Are your taxes too high?
Are you frustrated with the mind numbing complexity of the tax rules?

If so, this book is for you.

Taxes are the biggest expense for most people, especially for anyone in business. We work hard to earn an honest living, but it is not how much we earn that is important, it's how much we keep. Keeping more of what we earn means lowering taxes.

I can't promise that you will pay zero taxes, because most times that is not legally possible, but I can show you how to reduce your taxes to the legal minimum. I can't promise that you'll never be audited, but I can show you how to minimize the chances of being audited and how to protect yourself if you are audited.

You can practice financial offense and financial defense. Financial offense is working harder to earn and receive more money. Try as hard as we can there is no guarantee.

However financial defense is keeping what you have already made. Using *ProActive* tax saving strategies is one of the best ways of keeping what you have already earned. Just think of what you could use an extra few thousand dollars a year for! Money is not worth anything by itself—it's what you can do with it that matters. The vacation or the college education for your children—this is really what it is all about. Keeping more money in your pocket instead of losing it to the tax authorities is the best form of financial defense!

"The hardest thing in the world to understand is income taxes."

Albert Einstein

"On filing tax returns: this is too difficult for a mathematician, it takes a philosopher."

Albert Einstein

What is covered and what is not covered

The purpose of this book is to empower you to reduce your income taxes to the absolute legal minimum. I believe that anyone can, and should, understand enough to get along. Anyone can understand enough of how income taxes work. Like driving a car, we absolutely must know certain things to drive safely, but there are lots of things happening under the hood that we don't want to, or need to know. Focusing only on the essentials allows us to zero in, like a laser beam, on the things that really matter. We need to protect ourselves from the risk of getting overwhelmed!

It is my goal to give you enough information, but no more than enough, to control your income taxes. This book is not a cookbook with detail instructions. Because tax rules change so quickly, detail advice would soon be outdated—outright harmful as well as useless. The detail information would be perishable, but the overall principles are of more enduring benefit. I expect you will need to get more information, from trusted advisors, technical resources or both. The secret to reaching our goals is to understand the basics, only enough to get by, and leave the details to others.

I have refrained from getting into detail explanations of terms in the body of the text. Also, I have limited the use of tax code sections and case titles. They may be impressive, but most people won't use them anyway and those who are interested can readily find the information in a library or on the world-wide web.

This book takes into consideration rules that existed when it was written in May 2014. Because tax rules are constantly changing, there is the real risk that something here will have changed because of subsequent events. The reader should keep this in mind before implementing anything. I focus on broad concepts that do not change as frequently as the more specific rules.

"Government's view of the economy could be summed up in a few short phrases:
If it moves, tax it.
If it keeps moving, regulate it.
And if it stops moving, subsidize it."

Ronald Reagan

Part One

Tax Fundamentals

What You Need to Know

Numbers *matter, but not in the way you think!*

"Taxes are as much about *the meaning of words as about numbers."*

Edward Lyon, Esq. Principle
and Founder of Tax Coach Software

The Internal Revenue Service says that our tax system is voluntary; moreover, if you don't volunteer you can go to jail.

"There are known knowns. These are things we know that we know.
There are known unknowns. That is to say, there are things that we know we don't know.
But there are also unknown unknowns. There are things we don't know we don't know."

Donald Rumsfeld

Chapter 1: Overview of Taxes

There are all kinds of taxes; many of them lurk below the level of our consciousness. If there is a way to measure something (property or an activity) the government has found or will find a way to tax it.

> *According to Black's Law Dictionary, a tax is a "pecuniary burden laid upon individuals or property owners to support the government ... a payment exacted by legislative authority." It "is not a voluntary payment or donation, but an enforced contribution, exacted pursuant to legislative authority" and is "any contribution imposed by government ... whether under the name of toll, tribute, tallage, gabel, impost, duty, custom, excise, subsidy, aid, supply, or other name."*

Yes, the tax system is about raising money, but it is just as much about influencing our behavior as about raising money; the government uses the tax system for social engineering, to micromanage our behavior. The government offers to reduce taxes if we do certain things or threatens us with higher taxes or penalties for doing or not doing certain things. And this aspect of the tax system is getting more prominent. For instance, the new health care law will use the tax system to implement and enforce the penalty provisions and employer mandates; the government wants to encourage us to save for retirement so our taxes are reduced if we put money into retirement accounts.

Also, the tax system is always in flux, it is a very dynamic creature changing each and every minute as new laws are passed, new regulations are written and new court decisions come down. In addition to federal and state income taxes, there are also a slew of state and local taxes to contend with. Each state and local jurisdiction has its own tax laws.

When looking at tax reduction strategies we have to consider the entire range of taxes because we may reduce one tax but cause another to increase. When most people hear the word, "tax" they think of income taxes. This is an oversimplification. Appendix A has a more detail list of common taxes.

The focus of this book is on federal taxes found on the federal individual income tax return (form 1040) and to a lesser extent on the various business tax returns (forms 1120, 1120S, and 1065) that affect people in business. I do not delve deeply into corporate taxes because that would needlessly complicate the discussion.

Congress writes federal tax laws, which become part of the Internal Revenue Code (the Code). The Code is Title 26 of the United States Code. The laws passed by Congress are not detailed enough to be implemented—even though one would not think this from reading the code—so Congress delegates that responsibility to the Internal Revenue Service (IRS), a part of the Treasury Department. The IRS enforces the Code by writing rules, regulations, and other communications and preparing tax forms for us to fill out. There are books written just on how to understand the significance of IRS communications. In addition, the various federal courts decide cases involving tax laws and IRS rules and regulations. I will refer to this complex system of tax authority as "rules." In addition, as if this were not complicated enough, the IRS employs thousands of people that interact with taxpayers to enforce the rules. Each of these individuals has their own biases and quirks; they are people, not machines, even though they work for the IRS. I've seen cases where IRS personnel refuse to abide by their own rules taking the attitude: I've got my mind made up, don't confuse me with the facts! To be fair I have seen many cases where auditors went out of their way to give taxpayers a chance to present their position.

Congress may write tax laws but the laws frequently involve family relationships and the ownership of property. However, the individual states decide these issues, not the federal government. The federal government must defer to the individual states' laws, most notably when the issue concerns the ownership of property and family relationships. This was recently highlighted when Congress passed the Defense of Marriage Act that refused tax benefits to same sex married couples even though they were married according to state laws. The Supreme Court of the United States recently struck down the federal law because it encroached on matters reserved to the states to decide.

"Democracy must be something more than two wolves and a sheep voting on what to have for dinner."

James Bovard

"The art of taxation consists of so plucking the goose as to achieve a maximum of feathers with the minimum of hissing"

Colbert, finance minister to Louis XIV

Chapter 2: How The Tax System Operates

What if everything you thought about taxes were wrong?

Overview

Tax rules are either objective or subjective. Objective tax rules have bright line tests. They are fact based. Something is there or it is not there; there is no in-between, there is very little ambiguity. If you receive a form W-2 from your employer for your wages, it states exactly how much income should be included on your tax return. Either you included it on your tax return or you didn't. On the other hand, many tax rules are more subjective; that is they depend on personal perspective, feelings, beliefs, or desires as opposed to those made from independent objective facts. For example, there is no bright line test to determine whether or not someone is engaged in a "trade or business." But it makes a world of difference, for there are many tax advantages to being in a "trade or business." However, despite this lack of clear standards there are factors to consider, which, when evaluated as a whole, allow one to resolve the question. The factors need to be considered in conjunction with your individual facts and circumstances.

Taxpayers need to be aware of the factors that will be used to judge their activities and to make sure that they meet the criteria that allow them to come within rules which will result in lower taxes or no taxes at all. If the criteria aren't met, or there is ambiguity, you may get into an expensive battle of wits with the tax authorities. A battle which, even if you win on the merits, you will very likely lose because of the expense of defending yourself. These are the facts on the ground.

Thus, taxpayers must be co-creators of their tax reality and create the facts and circumstances that will allow them to create a reality less taxing than alternatives.

How you receive and spend your money makes all the difference in how much tax you pay or whether you even pay any tax. People in business have more control over how they receive their money and how they spend their money than most people. This is where the tax saving opportunities are found; by design, the design of Congress, the tax system is as much about how to keep money from taxation as it is about taxing income.

The amount of your income tax is based on taxable income. The amount of income tax is determined from a tax rate schedule published by the IRS. There are different tax rate schedules; the one you use depends on your marital status, and in addition, there is one for people who qualify as "head of household." The tax rate schedules are progressive, meaning that the higher your taxable income the greater the percentage you pay in tax. For 2014 income tax rates go from 10% to 39.6%. For instance, in 2014 a single person will owe 10% on their first $9,075 of taxable income; 15% on their taxable income between $9,076 and $36,900; 25% on their taxable income between $36,901 and $89,350; 28% on their taxable income between $89,351 and $186,350; 33% on their taxable income between $186,351 and $405,100; 35% on their taxable income between $401,101 and $406,750; and 39.6% on their taxable income over $406,750. Their total tax will be the sum of these amounts.

In addition to the tax tables there is something called the Alternative Minimum Tax (AMT) which is just another way of figuring your tax obligation. You pay the higher of the AMT or the amount determined from the tax schedules. The new healthcare act imposes additional taxes on investment income (3.8%) and earned income (.9%) if your income is greater than $200,000 for single taxpayers or $250,000 for married taxpayers. And if this weren't confusing enough the government takes back some deductions when your income exceeds certain amounts. I think of these as take backs. So, you see that tax rates can actually be much greater than indicated by just looking at the tax tables mentioned above.

In addition, there are other taxes we pay through the personal income tax return. I only want to mention one, one that many self-employed people run across: the self-employment tax. Are you familiar with the social security taxes withheld from your paycheck if you work for someone? Up to certain limits of income, the employer withholds a total of 7.65% for social security taxes from the employee and the employer also pays the same amount; for a total of 15.3%. Since a self-employed person doesn't have an employer he gets to pay a comparable tax called the self-employment tax that is 15.3% of self-employment income up to certain limits. Many self-employed people are surprised when they run across this for the first time.

So, how do you arrive at this thing called "taxable income"? I will give you a brief outline and then delve more deeply into each of the components.

So the really important question, the really interesting question is: how do you get to taxable income? Here is a summary. Go to the IRS website to take a look at the actual government forms.

+ Income received; items such as (the summary numbers are shown on form 1040, page one):

- Wages
- Interest and dividends (the total from 1040, Schedule B if you receive more than $400)
- Business income (or losses)—after subtracting expenses to earn the income (the total from form 1040, Schedule C)

- Capital gains (or losses); generally sales of property held for investment (the total from form 1040, Schedule D)
- Individual retirement accounts, pensions and annuities
- Rents and royalty income (or losses)—after subtracting expenses to earn the income (the total from form 1040, Schedule E)

= **Gross Income**

— **Adjustments to Gross Income**; this is a catch-all for various items, some related to income we earn as an employee and some items represent tax benefits for behavior that congress wants to encourage; items such as

- Educator expenses; $250 deduction if you are a school teacher and spend money for supplies
- Money put into health savings accounts
- Moving expense for employees
- Self-employed health insurance—you get to deduct it here rather than on Schedule A (see below)
- 50% of self-employment tax. This is intended to put you on par with the incorporated business that pays and deducts their 50%
- Retirement plan contributions

= **Adjusted Gross Income (AGI)**; this is an important number because it is used as a benchmark to calculate other tax deductions

— Subtractions from Adjusted Gross Income:

- Standard or itemized deductions; the standard deduction helps establish a threshold of income below which taxpayers who do not itemize will not be taxed in order to meet basic living expenses. It is a fixed amount that may be deducted without proof of actual expenses[1]; if the total is greater than the standard deduction, taxpayers can itemize (list them individually) their deductions. Itemized deductions consist of a number of specified items that may be deducted, that require substantiating evidence. Itemized deductions fall into the following categories (the total of itemized deductions comes from form 1040, Schedule A):
  - Medical expenses; to the extent that they are greater than 10% (7% if age 65 or older) of AGI
  - State and local taxes (including property taxes)
  - Interest paid on loans secured by your residence (subject to limits) or for loans used to purchase investments
  - Charitable contributions, either in cash or property
  - Miscellaneous itemized deductions, such as investment expenses, work expenses that are greater than 2% of AGI
- Personal exemptions also help establish a threshold of income below which taxpayers will not be taxed in order to meet basic living expenses. Because family size affects the ability of households to pay taxes, taxpayers may claim a deduction for themselves and for qualifying dependents. The exemption amount is adjusted each year for inflation. For 2014 each exemption amounts to $3,950.

= **Taxable Income**: This number is used to compute income tax as explained above.

---

[1] For 2014 the standard deduction is $6,200 for single taxpayers; $12,400 for married taxpayers filing joint returns ($6,200 if filing separately); and $9,100 for head of households.

The balance of tax owed or overpaid is determined as follows:
Tax computed based on taxable income as described above
— Non-refundable credits, such as:

- Foreign tax credit
- Credit for child and dependent care expense
- Education credits
- Child tax credit

+ Other taxes, such as:

- Self-employment tax
- Penalty for premature withdrawal from retirement plans

— Payments and refundable tax credits:

- Income tax withheld by employers and others
- Estimated tax payments
- Child tax credit
- Excess social security tax paid (such as from multiple employers)

= Tax underpaid (e.g. balance due) or overpaid (e.g. refund)

Business and rental property activities

Income is economic gain or profit from an activity. Therefore, you need to subtract the costs and expenses of earning that income to figure the amount subject to taxation.

> *There shall be allowed as a deduction all the ordinary and necessary expenses paid or incurred during the taxable year in carrying on any trade or business, including a reasonable allowance for salaries or other compensation for personal services actually rendered; traveling expenses (including amounts expended for meals and lodging other than amounts which are lavish or extravagant under the circumstances) while away from home in the pursuit of a trade or business; and rentals or other payments required to be made as a condition to the continued use or possession, for*

purposes of the trade or business, of property to which the taxpayer has not taken or is not taking title or in which he has no equity. [2]

In addition, Internal Revenue Code Section 62 allows Deductions Attributable To Rents And Royalties

Now compare the above with the rule for personal living expenses.

Except as otherwise expressly provided in this chapter (Author's comment: this relates mainly to items allowed as itemized deductions), no deduction shall be allowed for personal, living, or family expenses. [3]

Tax tip:
Make your pleasurable activities into a business; just operate the activity with the intention of making a profit and be prepared to prove it! Why not have fun while you're making money and let Uncle Sam be your partner.

This sounds simple, but dig a little deeper and ask yourself: What is a trade or business? This is a critically important question to answer. Because personal living expenses are usually not deductible, but business expenses are frequently deductible. And understanding this seemingly simple concept opens the doors to tax saving opportunities.

A trade or business is an activity which is carried on with continuity and regularity to make a profit. An activity that is merely sporadic, or that constitutes a hobby or an amusement or diversion is not a trade or business.

Trade or business expenses must meet three tests. First, the expenses must be related to a trade or business. Second, the expenses must be ordinary and necessary. Third, the expenses

---

[2] Internal Revenue Code Section 162
[3] Internal Revenue Code Section 262

must be paid or incurred in carrying on a trade or business. There are limitations on deducting certain expenses, but you must meet these tests first. For instance, the cost of capital expenditures (assets that have a useful life greater than one year) is sometimes deducted over the future years. This is called depreciation. However, special rules may allow deductions earlier.

Passive Activities

In 1986 Congress, in response to perceived abuses by rich taxpayers deducting losses from tax shelters, passed the passive activity rules. In general, these rules say that taxpayers can only deduct losses and expenses from passive activities from income that comes from passive activities. In other words, losses and expenses from passive activities cannot reduce income from non-passive sources such as salary, interest, and dividends. A passive activity is a trade or business in which the taxpayer does not participate. By definition, any rental property is a passive activity. However, there are special exceptions for real estate rental activities and real estate professionals. Any loss from a passive activity not allowed for the year incurred is suspended and carried forward until the activity is disposed of or there is passive activity income.

A taxpayer materially participates in an activity if the taxpayer participates in the business on a regular, continuous, or substantial basis. There are seven tests for material participation:

1. 500-Hour Test: If the taxpayer participates for more than 500 hours during the tax year, or
2. 100-Hour Test: If the taxpayer participates for more than 100 hours during the tax year, and that individual's participation is no less

> Taxpayers can't rely on IRS employees to know the rules. More than once, I have had audit situations where the IRS agents wanted to disallow my client's loss from a rental property. Each time I had to show them how one of these rules applied to my client. They were finally convinced, but it took some effort!

than the participation of any other individual, or

3. Substantially All Test: If the taxpayer's participation constitutes substantially all of the participation in the activity of all individuals for the tax year, or
4. Significant Participation Activity (SPA): If the activity is a SPA and the individual's aggregate participation in all SPA's exceeds 500 hours. An activity is an SPA if the individual participates for more than 100 hours during the tax year, or
5. Five Out of Ten-Year Test: Uses material participation in prior years to determine whether the taxpayer materially participated in the current year; if the taxpayer materially participated for any five of the preceding 10 taxable years, or
6. Three-Year Test for a Personal Service Activity: If the taxpayer materially participated in the activity for any three prior taxable years, or
7. Facts and Circumstances Test: The above six tests are quantitative. This test is a subjective one that allows a taxpayer to establish material participation by showing—based on all the facts and circumstances—the individual's participation in the activity was regular, continuous, and substantial.

Exception for Real Estate Professionals: If the taxpayer is a real estate professional, the passive activity rules do not apply to rental real estate activities in which they materially participate according to the above rules.[4]

A taxpayer is a real estate professional if:

1. More than half of the personal services performed by the taxpayer in trades or businesses during the tax year are performed in "real property trades or businesses " in which the taxpayer materially participates; and
2. The taxpayer performs more than 750 hours of services during the tax year in real property trades or businesses in which they materially participate.

Special rule that allows certain taxpayers to deduct up to $25,000 of losses from rental real estate:[4] A taxpayer can deduct up to $25,000 of losses from rental real estate activities in which they actively participate against non-passive income. The $25,000 is reduced by 50% of the taxpayer's adjusted gross income greater than $100,000. So the deduction is completely phased-out when adjusted gross income reaches $150,000.

The taxpayer actively participates if they participate in making management decisions or arranging for others to provide service in a significant and bona fide manner. This is a less stringent standard than the material participation standard discussed above.

Alternative Minimum Tax

The Alternative Minimum Tax is, as the name implies, an alternative way of figuring your tax obligation. It disallows certain items which are allowed in the regular tax calculation. The calculation starts with the regular tax taxable income and adds back things which are not allowed for the alternative tax. There

---

[4] For California, there is no such exception!

are several items that are disallowed, but the ones that trap most people are personal deductions, state and local income taxes, the bargain element of incentive stock options, and unreimbursed employee business expenses and miscellaneous itemized deductions.

The resulting number is called the Alternative Minimum Taxable Income from which an exemption amount is subtracted to arrive at the amount subject to the Alternative Minimum Tax. A special tax rate schedule is used to arrive at the Alternative Minimum Tax. You pay the higher of the Regular Tax or the Alternative Minimum Tax.

Capital Gains and Losses

There are special rules, including special tax rates that apply to capital gains and losses. So what is a capital asset?

A capital asset is "property held by the taxpayer," but excludes the following eight classes of property:

1. Inventory or other property held primarily for sale to customers in the ordinary course of the taxpayer's trade or business;
2. Depreciable or real property used in the taxpayer's trade or business;
3. Certain literary or artistic property;
4. Accounts or notes receivable arising from the taxpayer's trade or business;
5. Certain publications of the federal government;
6. Commodities derivative financial instruments held by commodities derivatives dealers;
7. Hedging transactions; and
8. Supplies of a type regularly consumed in the ordinary course of the taxpayer's trade or business.

The tax on the sale or exchange of capital assets held (owned) for less than one year (these are called short-term) is different than for those held for one year or more (these are called long-term). Short-term capital gains are taxed at ordinary income tax rates. Most long-term gains (there are exceptions) are taxed at lower rates.

Capital Gains: Special Tax Rates

- 20% if the taxpayer is in the 39.6% income tax bracket;
- 15% if the taxpayer is in the 25%, 28%, 33%, or 35% income tax bracket; or
- zero if the taxpayer is in the 10% or 15% income tax bracket.
- A 25% tax rate is imposed on long-term capital gain attributable to certain prior depreciation that was claimed on real property (recaptured Section 1250 gain)

These rates apply for both the regular tax and the minimum tax.

To determine whether there is a capital gain or loss and its character as short-term or long-term the short-term gains or losses and the long-term gains and losses are combined. The character of the resulting gain or loss is determined by the larger of the short-term or long-term items.

If there is a net loss it can offset other income items only up to $3,000 and any excess is carried forward to be used in the future until used up.

> **Tax tip:** If you want to reduce your taxable estate, give away property up to the annual exclusion amount each year. You can give away individual property or interests in a family limited partnership.

Estate and Gift Taxes

Most people are surprised to learn that there is a tax levied on people who give their property away—either during their lifetime or at death. The government doesn't have enough revenue agents to go after kids that give away unwanted lunches at school, so there is a an amount of property you can give away each year and not have to report it. Called the gift tax annual exclusion amount, it is $14,000 (adjusted yearly for inflation) for 2014. A person can give away property valued at up to $14,000 per donee (the person who receives the gift) per year.

The estate tax is a tax levied on the fair market value of property transferred at death—other than to one's spouse. For decedents dying in 2014, property with a fair market value up to $5,340,000 is not taxed. The fair market value of property above this amount is taxed at 40%.

Inherited property gets, what is called, a step-up in basis to the value at the date of death. The person who inherits property uses that value at date of death to determine their gain or loss if they sell the property. In other words, the increase in value during the time the property was held by the decedent is not taxed.

Other Taxes

Self-employment tax

A self-employed individual is subject to self-employment tax. A person is self-employed if they carry on a trade or business as a sole proprietor or independent contractor. The tax is imposed on net self-employment income. However, note that income from rental real estate activities, even though the activity may be considered a business, is not subject to self-employment tax.

The tax is made up of three components: 1) 12.4% of net self-employment income for Social Security (old-age, survivors, and disability insurance) on income up to an amount which is adjusted yearly. The limit for 2014 is $117,000, 2) 2.9% for Medicare (hospital insurance) on all net self-employment income, and 3) for tax years beginning after 2012 the Medicare portion of the self-employment tax rate is increased by an additional 0.9% (to 3.8%) for self-employment income greater than $200,000 for single individuals or $250,000 for a married couple filing a joint return ($125,000 if they file separate tax returns).

Penalties

- Underpayment of estimated tax: you are supposed to pay-in your tax either through withholding by an employer or through quarterly payments, known as estimated tax payments. There may be a penalty if you don't pay-in enough.
- Early withdrawal from retirement plans: Taxable distributions from a qualified retirement plan or an Individual Retirement Account (IRA) are subject to a 10% additional tax (2½% for California) if they are made before the participant reaches ager 59½. There are certain exception to the penalty, most notable for:
  - Distributions rolled-over into another plan
  - Distributions upon death or disability of the participant
  - Distributions after separation from service that are part of a series of periodic payments
  - Distributions not exceeding deductible medical expenses or
  - Certain qualified first-time homebuyer distributions.

Tax Credits

Credits are dollar for dollar reductions in your tax liability. Most credits will only offset the current year's tax, but some of them are refundable—meaning that you get the money back even if you have no tax obligation.

A tax deduction, on the other hand, will only reduce your tax by the amount of your tax rate. For instance, if you have a $1,000 personal deduction and your federal tax rate is 25%, the deduction will save you $250. Therefore, the higher your tax rate the more tax deductions are worth to you.

Some of the more common credits:

1. Adoption credit
2. Earned income tax credit (refundable)
3. Education credits
4. Low income housing credit
5. Child and dependent care credit
6. Child tax credit
7. Foreign tax credit

"You're free to choose what you do,
but you're not free to choose the consequences."

Fred Thompson

"If you don't take control of change,
change will take control of you."

Fred Thompson

"Day in and day out, your tax accountant can make or lose you more money than any single person in your life, with the possible exception of your kids."

Harvey Mackay

Part Two

How to Save Taxes

By failing to prepare, you are preparing to fail.

Benjamin Franklin

Any one may so arrange his affairs that his taxes shall be as low as possible; he is not bound to choose that pattern which will best pay the Treasury; there is not even a patriotic duty to increase one's taxes. Gregory v. Helvering, 69 F.2d 809, 810 (2d Cir. 1934)

Over and over again courts have said that there is nothing sinister in so arranging one's affairs as to keep taxes as low as possible. Everybody does so, rich or poor; and all do right, for nobody owes any public duty to pay more than the law demands: taxes are enforced exactions, not voluntary contributions. To demand more in the name of morals is mere cant. Commissioner v. Newman, 159 F.2d 848, 851 (2d Cir. 1947) - dissenting opinion

"If you fail to plan,
you plan to fail."

Fred Thompson

"What gets measured gets managed."

Fred Thompson

Chapter 3: Basics of Tax Saving Strategies

As the above quote indicates the key to saving taxes, reducing taxes to the absolute legal minimum is *ProActive* tax planning! And there are a multitude of ways to reduce taxes if you are in business; but if you do not take the initiative, the government has a default plan and the default plan usually results in higher taxes. Tax burdens are dependent on the source of income, how it is paid and how it is used. You can lower your taxes by managing these variables.

Clients tell me that they want me to prepare their tax returns so that there is no risk. What they mean is no risk that there could be adverse audit findings. However, there is another risk to look out for—the risk of paying too much tax, the risk of paying more than you legally owe. I tell them that the 99% risk free plan is to pay tax on everything of value that they receive during the year and take no deductions. Notice that I didn't say that this is 100% risk free but only 99% risk free; because there is always something the government can question! When taxpayers learn what the 99% risk-free plan will cost them in terms of higher taxes they always decide that some risk is better than the risk of paying too much tax.

In general, anything of value that you receive is taxable and there are no deductions—unless you can point to a tax rule that says otherwise. This means that you have the burden to show that something of value received is not subject to tax and that something is tax deductible. The important point to remember is that it is up to you to take the initiative. The taxpayer has the burden of proof.

The question each person must answer is; how much risk are they willing to take on? This is easiest to understand by putting it in the context of the risk versus reward tradeoff. Everyone has their own tolerance for risk and their own evaluation of reward. It is important to evaluate the potential rewards and balance them against the potential risks. The reward should be greater than the risks. In addition, you should not use a strategy that you are not comfortable with, no matter how much money you save. Rewards and risks are not only about money; they are also intangible emotional/psychic. You may be making lots of money, but if you can't sleep at night, it isn't worth it.

In addition to the risk versus reward issue, it is important to examine the benefit versus cost trade-offs. Tax strategies usually have costs to implement and costs to maintain them; sometimes the cost is small, but sometimes the cost can be high. A good tax strategy will be one that has an acceptable amount of risk and the tax savings will be greater than the costs.

When is something paid? If you're on the cash basis, as most taxpayers are, it's when you release a check or pay by credit card that is issued by a third party (e.g. not a store credit card). If the credit card is issued by a third party the item is considered paid for when you make the charge, not when you pay the credit card bill. Because you have incurred a liability to a third party. If you're short of cash at the end of the year and need tax deductions this may help.

Tax reduction cannot be the sole motive for doing something. If it is, the IRS can deny the related tax benefit. In technical terms, there must be economic substance for doing something for it to be valid. In other words, there must be a real valid reason for doing something other than saving taxes. Tax saving can be one of the reasons for doing something, but it can't be the only reason. This said it is usually easy to find a valid economic reason to do something; it is a matter of documenting the reason to preclude the IRS from attacking the transaction due to lack of economic substance. For example if you wanted to sell your house to your wholly owned corporation to recognize a gain, say to offset losses, tax saving would be a major motivator. But, you could document the fact that you are doing it for asset protection and estate planning reasons.

It is important to understand the distinction between tax avoidance and tax evasion because one is a legitimate way to saving taxes and the other is illegal and can subject you to criminal penalties; in other words jail time.

> *Any person who willfully attempts to evade or defeat any tax imposed by the internal revenue laws, or the payment of such taxes, is guilty of a felony and, upon conviction, may be fined not more than $250,000 ($500,000 in the case of a corporation) or imprisoned for not more than five years or both, together with the costs of prosecution. In addition, a civil fraud penalty may also be imposed.*
> *Internal Revenue Code Section 7201*

The elements of the crime of tax evasion are:
- A tax deficiency
- Affirmative act of evasion or attempt to evade tax; and
- Willfulness.

See Sansone v. U.S., 380 U.S. 343

Tax avoidance, on the other hand, is using legal means to lower or eliminate your tax obligation. Tax avoidance is legal.

Frequently there are different ways to structure activities. The courts have consistently reaffirmed the taxpayers' rights to structure their activities to reduce or eliminate taxes. Tax planning is the process of evaluating various legal ways of structuring activities to choose which is best; best from a tax as well as legal and economic standpoints.

> *Even according to the IRS "Payment of only the correct amount of tax. You are responsible for paying only the correct amount of tax due under the law—no more, no less."*
> *Internal Revenue Service Publication 17*

So how do you tell the difference between tax evasion and tax avoidance? Tax evasion frequently involves deceit, concealment, or distortion of the truth. Therefore, if you feel that you have to hide something to reduce taxes it more than likely involves illegal tax evasion—a crime that can land you in jail—rather than legal tax avoidance—a perfectly legal activity which can save thousands of dollars.

Chapter 4: General Strategies

Timing taxable income

Timing your taxable income refers to controlling the time when you receive income and pay expenses to lower your overall taxes. Notice I said overall taxes, by this I mean taxes that will be paid in the current year and in future years. Tax planning for 2012 was an interesting year because we knew that taxes were going up in 2013. Therefore, the usual strategy was reversed; it was better to accelerate taxable income into 2012 and pay the lower tax then rather than a higher tax in 2013.

Increase your taxable income, by accelerating income and deferring expenses, if you expect that your tax rate in the current year will be lower than your tax rate the following year, or if you need additional income in order to take advantage of an offsetting deduction or credit that will not be available in future tax years. Sometimes taxpayers have small amounts of income but relatively larger itemized deductions that will be lost if not used in the same tax year. I had a client who recently got divorced and had little income because she was caring for small children and had high mortgage interest on the house she was paying for. I learned that she had money in a traditional IRA. Over two years she was able to convert about $75,000 of money in her traditional IRAs into a Roth IRA. She paid no tax because she was able to use up her itemized deductions which otherwise would have been lost. She was able to convert taxable income (in the IRA) into tax-free income. Increase or decrease taxable income by:

- Converting regular individual retirement accounts (IRA) to a Roth IRA. You recognize income when you withdraw the IRA Thus recognizing income and using up deductions and turning taxable regular income from a regular IRA into non-taxable Roth IRA income.

- Reduce taxable income by deferring income and accelerate expenses. If you expect your tax rate to be the same this year and in the future and income will be higher this year than next year, or if you anticipate equal income in both years, you will benefit by deferring income until next year and accelerating expenses into this year. Thus putting off the tax obligation into the future.
- Strategies for itemized deductions
    - Bunching payments in one year—if your itemized deductions are always close to the standard deduction amount, try to pay all itemized deductions in one year to get above the standard deduction amount and then use the standard deduction in the other year.
    - Prepay state income taxes and property taxes if this will not cause you to fall into the alternative minimum tax (See below for more information)
    - Charitable Contributions: Consider making charitable contributions at the end of the year. Remember that you can make contributions of property as well as cash. It may pay to clean out your garage. Tax tip: if you are dealing with an estate, donate the unwanted personal property to charity; your basis (therefore you deduction) is the fair market value at the date of death!
    - Medical expenses: Bunch them by paying them all in one year, or paying them all next year to get over the 10% floor[5] or into years when AGI is lower.
    - Avoid phase-out of itemized deductions due to AGI limits by bunching itemized deductions into years when AGI is below the phase-out amounts. Itemized deductions are reduced when AGI is greater than $300,000 for married taxpayers filing joint ($150,000 if filing separate), $250,000 for single taxpayers, and

---

[5] For taxpayers overage 65 the floor is 7½% for tax years ending in 2013 through 2016.

$275,000 for those filing as head of household. Itemized deductions are reduced by 3% of the amount over these amounts up to 80% of itemized deductions. The following itemized deductions are not reduced: medical expenses; investment interest expense; and casualty, theft, or wagering losses.

- Rental property—opportunities to manage net income:
  - Prepay or defer expenses
  - Prepay property taxes: note that this doesn't affect the AMT
  - Purchase supplies before the end of the year instead of waiting until next year.

- Sole proprietorship
  - Defer income & accelerate expenses
    - Defer income—If you are on the cash basis, defer income by putting off the receipt of income until next year. If you are on the accrual basis put off completing work so that invoices are not sent out until the following year.
    - Accelerate expenses—If you are on the cash basis, pay expenses this year instead of next year. If you're on the accrual basis, incur expenses this year instead of next year. Even if you are on the cash basis, expenses that are financed may be deducted in the year in which the purchase is made when the financing is extended by someone other than the vendor. That is because the item is actually paid for by a third party. For example, credit card purchases (if the vendor does not issue the credit card), or an automobile (financed by an independent finance company).
    - Purchase supplies before the end of the year instead of waiting until next year.

        - Employee bonuses
        - Purchase equipment before the end of the year.
    - Accelerate income and defer expenses
        - Accelerate billing and collection of accounts receivable if you are on the cash basis.
        - Ask customers to pay for next year's goods or services in advance in the current year.
    - Wait until next year to pay expenses.

Shifting income to taxpayers in lower tax brackets

Give appreciated property to relatives in lower tax brackets. This works great to help children in college to pay for college expenses. The recipient's basis, in the case of appreciated property, is the same as the basis in the hands of the donor.

- **Advantage:**
  - The family unit pays less tax, and therefore has more money, than if the parent sold the property and paid out cash for the support;
  - In the case of a child that is in college, they may be able to use education credits if emancipated while parents frequently lose the benefits of education credits because of phase-outs for high income taxpayers.
- **How to implement**
  - Formally give the property and change title as appropriate;
  - File any gift tax returns.
- **Pitfalls**
  - Coordinate with estate planning;
  - May need to file gift tax returns;
  - Be sure that the property has appreciated. Because if there is a loss the recipient will not be able to recognize the loss. The recipient's basis is the lower of the basis in the hands of the donor or the fair market value of the property at the time of the gift.

Retirement Plans

The government wants to encourage us to save for our retirement so to encourage retirement saving it allows advantages for retirement savings; money put into a retirement account can be deducted from taxable income, and earnings on the funds in the retirement account are not taxed until withdrawn. The tax-free earnings is a big deal because you are earning money on the taxes that would otherwise be paid, both when the money was initially put in the account and the taxes on each years' earnings. This is like getting a free loan from the government. The money is supposed to be used for retirement so there is a penalty if you take the money out before retirement with certain exceptions (see below).

There is another type of retirement plan with a little difference—the Roth retirement account. The Roth account, established by the Taxpayer Relief Act of 1997, was named for Senator William Roth of Delaware its main sponsor. The different treatment is that the tax break is allowed when the money is taken out rather than when the money is put in the plan. There is no up-front tax deduction when money is put in the Roth account, but there is no tax on the earnings when money is taken out of the account. Money must be kept in the plan for a minimum period of time though. The Roth provides a better return when the advantage of the tax-free withdrawal of the Roth account at the end outweighs the advantage of the up-front tax deduction allowed by the more traditional retirement plans. This depends primarily on the amount of time funds are left in the account and the ultimate tax rate when the funds are taken out.

The Roth account allows opportunities for controlling your tax liability because you can convert a regular IRA to a Roth IRA without a penalty for early withdrawal on the regular IRA. In the year of the conversion, the amount converted is taxable income.

Example: I had a client with sizeable investments because of a divorce settlement. She had very little taxable income but she had itemized deductions from her home ownership. The itemized deductions, which totaled about $15,000, would be forever lost if not used—they don't carry forward! I learned that she had a lot of money in her regular IRA account. I suggested that she take some of the money out of her regular IRA, convert it to a Roth IRA, and report it as taxable income—just enough to use up her itemized deductions and pay zero tax. When she takes the money out of the Roth IRA there will be no tax. She effectively converted taxable regular IRA income to non-taxable income. We were able to do this for two years and saved taxes of about $15,000. Money she can now use for her retirement instead of giving it to the tax man. Pro-Active tax planning put $15,000 in her pocketbook.

There are two types of retirement plans 1) Qualified retirement plans and 2) Non-qualified retirement plans. Qualified retirement plans must comply with requirements to set-up separate trusts to provide retirement benefits. These are set-up by employers for their employees.

1) Qualified retirement plans: These are formal plans set-up by an employer for the benefits of employees. A self-employed person is considered, for this purpose, an employee of their sole proprietorship. To set-up a qualified plan the employer must prepare formal plan documents and may need to file tax returns for the plan. In addition, qualified plans must cover all eligible employees.

2) Retirement Saving Accounts: These are typically set-up and managed by a financial institution, however this is not always the case. The financial institution has the responsibility to file all the paperwork and comply with government regulations. These plans are known as Individual Retirement Accounts (IRA) or Roth Individual Retirement Accounts (Roth IRA).

See appendixes F and G for contribution limits.

Transferring between retirement account or Roll Overs: Generally, an individual may withdraw assets of a qualified plan or an IRA and exclude the withdrawal from income if the assets are transferred into another retirement plan. The rollover must be accomplished within 60 days after the withdrawal. This can be done only once a year.

Alternative Minimum Tax

Items that are treated differently for alternative minimum tax (AMT) purposes than for regular tax purposes and some suggestions.

1. Incentive stock options (IS0); the bargain element is considered income for the AMT. Before exercising ISO's, determine the tax consequences. To avoid or reduce AMT sell the stock in the year of exercise, or spread the exercise over a number of years.
2. State taxes are not deductible (e.g. income taxes, sales taxes, real and personal property taxes). Time the payment of state taxes so that they will not be paid in years that you will be subject to the AMT.
3. Unreimbursed employee business expenses and miscellaneous itemized deductions are not deductible for the AMT. Time the payment of unreimbursed business expenses and miscellaneous itemized deductions (such as deductible legal expenses) so that they will not be paid in years that

you will be subject to the AMT. If possible, have your employer reimburse you for employee business expenses.

4. Medical expenses must exceed 10% of AGI rather than 7.5% for taxpayers who are at least age 65. Take advantage of a pre-tax medical cafeteria plan if your employer offers one. If you pay medical bills through the plan, the diverted income no longer is included in taxable wages, and the medical expenses are no longer itemized deductions.
5. Personal exemptions are not allowed for the AMT. You may be able to arrange it so that dependents, such as college students, with modest taxable income, file their own separate tax returns claiming their personal exemptions.
6. Tax exempt bond income from private activity bonds is taxable for the AMT. If you want to invest in tax-exempt bonds, consider ones that are not private activity bonds.

Business Entities

There are various types of business entities you can use to operate your business.

- **Sole proprietorship:** A sole proprietorship is a type of business entity that is owned and run by one individual There is no legal distinction between the owner and the business. The owner receives all profits and has unlimited responsibility for all debts. This is the default form of business if another one is not used.

- **Partnership:** A partnership is the relationship existing between two or more persons who join together to carry on a trade or business. There are two types of partnerships, the general partnership and the limited partnership.

  In a general partnership, all of the partners manage the business and each of the partners has joint and several liability for the debts of the partnership. This means that each of the partners is responsible for the liabilities of the partnership. A limited partnership, on the other hand has a partner or partners that operate the business, take responsibility for the liabilities of the partnership and have limited partners. The limited partners do not operate the business and their liability is limited to their capital accounts.

For income tax reporting purposes, a partnership is treated as a collection of individuals, each of which reports their respective share of the partnership's tax attributes. A partnership is often called a "flow through entity" because the tax attributes flow through to the partners.

> **Caution:** If corporate formalities are not respected a court may determine that justice requires disregarding the corporation and hold the owners personally responsible. This is called "piercing the corporate veil."

- **Corporation:** A corporation is an entity created by the law of the state in which it is organized. Shareholders in a corporation are not liable for corporate debts. This is the most important attribute of a corporation compared to a sole proprietorship or a general partnership. A corporation is a legal entity separate from the owners. Because a corporation is an artificial entity the shareholders and directors are required to treat it as if it were a separate person with its own interests apart from the owners. Therefore, they should memorialize significant corporate decisions in the corporate records. They should respect corporate formalities by creating minutes of meetings and written agreements between the corporation and related parties such as shareholders and directors.

For tax purposes, a corporation is treated as separate tax paying entity by default. However, a corporation that meets certain criteria, can elect to be treated as a partnership for tax purposes.

This is called Subchapter S tax treatment because the rules are found in Subchapter S of the Internal Revenue Code. The corporation is treated as a flow through entity. If the owner/employees of the S Corporation take money (distributions) out of the corporation it is supposed to be reported as salary up to the fair market value for their services. Any remaining profits flow through to the shareholders subject only to income tax, not employment taxes.

- **Limited Liability Company (LLC):** This is a new form of business organization. It combines the personal liability protection of a regular corporation with the simplicity of operations of a partnership. An LLC may be taxed as a sole proprietorship, a partnership, or a corporation depending on the number of owners and the election of the owners. If the owners don't do anything, a single member LLC is disregarded for tax purposes and taxed as a sole proprietorship, an LLC with more than one member is treated as a partnership. An LLC can elect to be taxed as a corporation and the corporation can elect S Corporation tax treatment.

See Appendix E for an analysis of business goals and how the various business entities can help achieve your goals.

"America is a land of taxation that was founded to avoid taxation."

Dr. Lawrence J. Peter

"The difference between death and taxes is death doesn't get worse every time Congress meets."

Will Rogers

"Thinking is one thing no one has ever been able to tax."

Charles Kettering

Chapter 5: Tax strategies For Individuals

Rescue tax-free gain on sale of your personal residence

If you sell your personal residence that you have owned and occupied for 24 months during the last five years, you do not have to pay tax on up to $250,000 ($500,000 if married) of the gain on the property.

If you are you about to lose the tax-free gain on sale of your residence due to lapse of time, sell to your wholly owned corporation or Limited Liability Company. You recognize the gain and still own the property through the corporation.

- **Advantage:**
    - Rescue tax-free income
- **How to implement**
    - Form your corporation or Limited Liability Company
    - Sell property and transfer title
- **Pitfalls**
    - Cost and trouble managing another entity

Rescue the tax loss on your personal residence

There is no tax deduction if you lose money when selling property used for personal purposes. However if you sell business or rental property you may be able to deduct the loss.

So if you have a loss on property used for personal purposes, turn it into rental or business property.

For instance, if you have a loss on your personal residence and want to dispose of it, first turn it into a rental property. A loss from selling your personal residence is considered personal and is not tax-deductible. A loss from selling a rental property is a capital loss and offsets capital gains or is tax-deductible up to $3,000 each year to offset other income. The amount not deducted is carried forward to use in future years.

- **Advantage:**
  - Turn non-deductible loss into a tax deductible loss
- **How to implement**
  - Use the property for business or rental uses. How do you prove the change of intent? There is not a bright line test, but you should be able to demonstrate from your actions that your purpose in owning the property has changed from personal to rental.

    Manifest your intent with tangible actions. For instance, rent the property for a long enough time to show that your intention is really to rent the property rather than just renting the property temporarily to mitigate expenses until you can sell it. Intent—an intangible thing which only exists in the mind—is proven by showing tangible things which demonstrate the intent. Don't tell—show!
- **Pitfalls**
  - The government may try to challenge the business or rental purpose for holding the property.

Chapter 6: Tax Strategies For Brokers And Agents

Employ children or other family members

Employ children or other family members who are in lower tax brackets in your business.

- **Advantage:**
    - You save tax on the difference in the tax rates between the business owner with the higher tax rate and the family member employed. The income tax rate and self-employment tax rates of the business owner can be as much as 60% while the children's tax rate may be zero or 10%. Therefore a salary of $20,000 to a child can reduce the family tax burden by $10,000
    - The money stays in the family unit
    - Work responsibilities give valuable life lessons to children and they can use the money for their extracurricular activities instead of the parent paying
    - Wages of children under age 18 employed by their parents in a sole proprietorship are not subject to social security tax.
- **How to implement:**
    - Must be a bonafide employer/employee relationship
    - Make sure that you keep meticulous records
    - File payroll records (e.g. payroll tax returns, year-end wage reports) if required
    - Keep track of hours worked
- **Pitfalls:** The IRS is skeptical of related party transactions so it is important to abide by all the formalities.

Lease real estate or equipment to your business

If your business uses real estate of equipment, own it outside of the business and lease it to the business.

- **Advantage:**
    - The business activity is subject to social security or self-employment taxes. So the lease deduction on the business reduces the amount subject to social security or self-employment taxes which are approximately 15.3% on income up to $117,000 (the maximum amount subject to social security in 2014) and 2.9% on income above this amount
    - The lease income reported on the individuals income tax returns is not subject to social security or self-employment taxes
    - Bingo, you just saved 15%
    - There are also asset protection advantages. For instance putting the asset in a corporation or a limited liability company isolates the asset from creditors of the business or the individual
    - Can also shift income to family members in lower tax brackets by giving them a share of the property or the business entity that owns the property
- **How to implement:**
    - Must be a bonafide lease, so prepare an agreement
    - Pay fair market value for the property
    - Make all payments according to the lease
    - Be sure to issue yearly tax information reports (form 1099)
- **Pitfalls:**
    - IRS may try to disallow the arrangement if formalities are not observed.

Medical expense reimbursement plan (MERP)
Employ the spouse in a business (other than an S Corporation or partnership) and pay for all employee health insurance and set up a medical expense reimbursement plan.

- **Advantage:**
    - Maximize medical expense deduction—avoid the limits to itemized deductions and the AMT limits;
    - The medical expenses are fully deductible as a business expense which also reduces self-employment tax;
    - Compensation can be solely in the form of medical expenses. If so, there is no need to report the payroll because it's considered non-taxable compensation!
- **How to implement:**
    - Must be a bonafide employee and document the same as you would for any unrelated employee;
    - Compensation in the form of money or benefits must be reasonable compensation.
- **Pitfalls:**
    - IRS may try to disallow the arrangement if formalities are not observed;
    - If cash wages are involved, need to withhold income taxes and pay employment taxes and file payroll tax returns

Home office expense
If a portion of your residence is used regularly and exclusively for your business, you can deduct the proportion of the common expenses (usually based on the relative square footage) of the home and all the direct expenses. Common expenses are those that relate to both the personal use and the business use. Direct expenses are those related solely to the business use.

This does not apply to rental of residence by employee to their employer during any period in which the employee uses the residence in performing services as an employee of the employer.

An independent contractor is treated as an employee per IRC 280A(c)(6).

See Appendix I for How to Deduct Home Office Used by Your Corporation

In the case of an employee, the home office must be for the convenience of the employer. If the home office expenses are not reimbursed by the employer, they are taken as an itemized deduction.

- **Advantage:**
  - Some otherwise nondeductible expenses for the residence become deductible business expenses;
  - Tax-deductible automobile expense is increased because the tax home is the home office and automobile mileage starts at the home office. Non-deductible commuting is from the residence to the home office—usually just a matter of feet.
- **How to implement:**
  - Be ready to prove the existence of the home office: take pictures of the home office; prepare a drawing of the floor plan showing the square footage.
  - Use the home office as the mailing address for the business to help demonstrate that home office is used for administrative functions.
- **Pitfalls:**
  - Is this a Red Flag? I frequently hear this—that people think taking the home office deduction is a red flag that will trigger an audit. This is not true! Several years ago this may have been true, but in 1990 the tax court decided *Soliman v. Com.*, 94 T.C. 20), Doctor Soliman challenged the IRS when they disallowed his home office. He lost the case but the court defined when a home office can be taken.

Subsequently Congress gave us Internal Revenue Code Section 280A which specifies when you can take home office expenses.

Travel, Meals and Entertainment

Travel Expenses:

You can deduct travel expenses related to your business activities. However, the Internal Revenue Service can summarily disallow travel expenses if you don't follow the documentation rules. Therefore, it is important to understand these rules and to keep the required documentation to get the tax deductions you deserve. Also, if you understand the rules, you can combine some personal/fun activities with a business trip and most of the cost of the trip will be tax deductible.

> ***Tax tip:***
> *Just because you are having fun doesn't mean it cannot be deducted. Combine pleasure with business correctly and you can deduct the travel.*

This is general information that addresses rules for the business owner. Most of the rules discussed here also pertain to the employee traveling but employees have less stringent documentation requirements.

Deductible travel expense (including transportation expense while in travel status) must be:

- Reasonable and necessary,
- Incurred while away from home, and
- In the pursuit of business.

Deductible travel expenses include—transportation (travel fares, vehicle expenses and so on); lodging; a portion of the cost of meals; incidental expenses.

> ***Tax tip:***
> *If business is greater than personal, all travel and business day expenses are deductible*
>
> *If personal is greater than business, travel is not deductible, but business day expenses, including lodging for business days is deductible*

In order to keep you from getting lost in a maze of information, I'm going to break down the information into the following topics:

1. Transportation expenses to/from a destination
2. Transportation expenses & business day expenses
3. Travel with your spouse and others
4. What is away from home
5. Documentation required

1. Transportation Expenses To/From a Destination

Only business travel is deductible. If the trip is for other than business purposes, the travel expenses are non-deductible personal expenses and the meals and lodging are non-deductible living expenses.

If you travel to a destination and engage in both business and personal activities, traveling expenses to and from such destination are deductible only if the trip is primarily business. If the trip is primarily personal in nature, the traveling expenses to and from the destination are not deductible even though you engage in business activities while at the destination.

Whether a trip is primarily business or is primarily personal depends on the facts and circumstances in each case. The amount of time spent on personal activities compared to the amount of time spent on business activities is a very important factor in determining whether the trip is primarily personal.

> Special Planning Note—Make sure that anytime you combine a business trip with personal/family days, that your primary purpose for the trip is business, and that you spend more days on business than personal pleasure.
>
> > The 51%/49% Transportation Rule:
> > When you travel within the 50 United States (including Washington, D.C.) and

spend more days (51% or more of your days on business than you spend on personal), you may deduct 100% of the cost of your transportation. However, if the purpose of the trip is not primarily for business (less than 51% of your days on business), you lose all of your transportation deduction for that trip.

2. Transportation Expenses & Business Day Expenses

Expenses "on-the-road" are divided into two categories—transportation expenses and business day expenses. 1) Transportation expenses are airfare, vehicle expenses, etc. to transport yourself while you are out-of-town, 2) Business day expenses are expenses at the destination such as eating and hotel rooms. You may deduct business expenses such as food and lodging even when your trip does not include enough business days to make it a business trip.

Special Problems In Figuring Business Days
Weekend, Holidays, and Standby Days: These days count as business days when they fall in-between business days during a business trip where it would not be practical to return home from your business destination over the weekend because of time required or expense involved.

Special Consideration for Saturday Night Travel: Because airlines often offer large discounts if your flight days span Saturday night, if you can save money (expenses) by staying over Saturday night you may count the stay-over days as business days.

Travel Days: Travel days count as business days, provided your point-to-point transit time plus business activity time for the day exceeds four hours.

Special Planning Note—If your trip is primarily business and you conduct business on Friday and the next Monday, the weekend in between will automatically count as business days as long as it was not practical for you to return home.

3. Travel With Your Spouse and Others

No deduction for travel of a spouse, dependent, or other individual accompanying you on business travel unless:

- The spouse, dependent, or other companion is your employee and;
- The travel of the spouse, dependent, or other companion is for a bona fide business purpose.

The law makes it clear that your spouse not only must be an employee of your business, but also must travel for a bona fide business purpose.

> Special Planning Note—If your spouse and/or others accompany you and their expenses are not deductible, make sure you reduce your deduction by the actual cost of their travel rather than let the IRS do so under audit. The IRS will probably make a ratable allocation to determine the non-deductible portion whereas the actual additional cost is probably much less!

4. What Is Away From Home?

The phrase "away from home" means that you must be away from your principal place of business (your tax home) overnight, or long enough to require sleep or rest.

The IRS only permits you to deduct expenses while away from your principal place of business, known as your tax home. Identifying your tax home is critical. Generally, your tax home is your principal place of business. You may deduct travel expenses while temporarily away from that home in the pursuit of business.

Generally, you will not be treated as being away from home if an assignment lasts more than one year. However, if you are employed for an indefinite or uncertain time at a distant work site, you cannot deduct living expenses at the distant job site even if it is inconvenient to move to the new location. In order to justify a deduction for living expenses while away from home at a distant job site, you must establish that:

- The new job is temporary;
- You maintain a residence in the vicinity of your principal business;
- You incur additional living expenses while away from home; and
- Travel is for business rather than personal reasons.

The IRS has ruled that a taxpayer without a principal place of business has a tax home at his personal residence if it is a "regular place of abode in a real and substantial sense." This ruling is important for traveling salesmen who often have no permanent place of business.

5. Documentation Required

> ***Tax tip:***
> *If your business is incorporated, you should have yearly board of directors meetings. Why not have them somewhere fun—in order to facilitate the conduct of business.*

To prove a business travel expenses you must have adequate records—you must maintain a diary or account book in which each expense item is recorded at or near the time of the expenditure. You must also maintain documentary evidence, such as paid bills or receipts, for lodging expenses away from home and any other items for $75 or more. Certain simplified methods of record keeping are permitted such as using a standard daily allowance for meals, incidentals and/or lodging. The Internal Revenue Service issues tables which provide allowable daily amounts according to the location. For example the allowable daily amount for lodging, meals and incidentals in Redwood City and San Mateo is currently $149. These amounts vary by location and change frequently.

The information that should appear in the diary or account book varies depending on the nature of the expense. It is not necessary to include information in a diary which is on a receipt so long as the diary and receipt complement each other in an orderly manner. You must be able to establish all of the following with respect to each trip away from home:

- Each separate amount for travel, lodging, and meals (although incidental items can be totaled in reasonable categories such as meals and taxi fares);
- The dates the you left and returned home for each trip, and the number of days spent on business activities;
- The travel destination, described by city name or other designation; and
- The business purpose for the travel or nature of the business benefit gained or expected as result of the trip unless the business purpose is obvious from the circumstances, (e.g., a salesman's regular sales calls).

Special Rule For Meals and Entertainment Expenses: Also, you must keep records to establish all of the following with respect to each meal and entertainment item:

- Each separate amount for meals and entertainment;
- The date of the meal or entertainment;
- The place of the meal, or the entertainment destination, described by name, address, and designation of type of entertainment, such as dinner or theater, if not apparent from the designation of the place;
- The business purpose for the meal or entertainment or the nature of the business benefit gained or expected as a result of the meal or entertainment,

unless the business purpose is obvious from the circumstances, and the nature of any business discussion or activity; and

- The business relationship to the you of the person at the meal or the person entertained, including their name, title, occupation or other designation sufficient to establish the business relationship to the you.

If you keep a copy of the receipt or charge slip from the restaurant, you will have most of this information. Just make a notation of the names of the people and their business relationship.

Meals and Entertainment

You can deduct meals and entertainment even if you are not travelling. For instance if you are showing houses to a client and stop for lunch together, you can deduct the cost of the meal. Also, you can deduct the cost of associated entertainment such as going to a concert or show. In addition to the documentation requirements for meals (see above) you will need to document that the entertainment took place immediately before or after a business interaction.

Generally meals and entertainment are 50% deductible. This came about several years ago because Congress wanted to curtail perceived abuses for those fat-cat business people having three martini lunches! However, meals or food offered to all employees or the public are 100% deductible. Be sure to tell your tax preparer or they will probably only deduct 50%.

Sell property that has a loss rather than trading it in

The like-kind exchange rules apply when business or rental property is traded-in for like kind property. Any gain or loss is not recognized, it is rolled into the replacement property. This is good in the case of property with a gain because it defers the gain until the replacement property is disposed of. However, this is not so good if the old property has a loss. It is generally best to recognize the loss as soon as possible because it may save taxes.

Instead of trading in business or rental property with a loss, sell it and recognize the loss immediately.

This may also be a good strategy if you have business or rental property with a gain if you have losses that can offset the gain.

Artificial creatures—Corporations and other entities created by the law

Use an S Corporation to minimize employment taxes

A corporation taxed under Subchapter S of the Internal Revenue Code is known as an S Corporation. Set-up an S Corporation to minimize self-employment taxes; minimize wages of the shareholders and thereby maximize the amount which flows through as income from the S corporation. The amount of profit in the S Corporation flows through to the shareholders and is taxed as ordinary income; this amount is not subject to employment taxes or self-employment taxes.

Many times I have seen employee shareholders of S corporations take all of the profits out of the business as salary. The employee shareholders are supposed to report money taken out of an S corporation as salary only up to the amount considered reasonable compensation. For the factors to consider in coming up with "reasonable compensation" see Appendix D.

- **Advantage:**
  - Eliminate employment taxes on profits passed through to the shareholders as net profits from the S Corporation.
- **How to implement:**
  - Determine how much is reasonable compensation and use this amount as the limit for money taken out reported as wages.
- **Pitfalls:**
  - The IRS may try to challenge the amount reported as wages, but this should not be a problem if you have considered the guidelines.

Chapter 7: Tax Strategies For Real Estate Investors

Trade property instead of selling it

If you want to get out of a property, consider trading it for another more desirable property instead of selling it. A sale is a taxable event while a trade is not taxable. If you want some cash consider borrowing the money using the property as security. Borrowed money is not taxable.

If you cannot find a property to trade for when you dispose of the relinquished property you can do what is called a deferred exchange, also known as a Starker exchange (named after the taxpayer who took this issue to court and won). If you receive property other than replacement property (called boot), you will recognize gain up to the amount of the boot received. The profit on the transfer of the relinquished property not recognized reduces your cost basis in the replacement property. If, and when you sell the replacement property you will recognize the profit if any.

You must identify the replacement property no later than the 45th day after the relinquished property is transferred and the replacement property must be received within 180 days or by the due date of the tax return for the year of the transfer, if earlier.

- **Advantage:**
  - Defers or completely eliminates tax on the disposition of property.
- **How to implement**
  - Need to use a middle-man (also known as a "straw man") to hold any proceeds from the relinquished property. The taxpayer cannot take control of any of the funds.

- **Pitfalls**
  - Need to comply with some complicated rules
  - Cost of the middle-man

Identify elements of property for faster write-off

A tax deduction today is more valuable than a tax deduction tomorrow. Property with a useful life that extends beyond the current tax year is written-off or depreciated (e.g. deducted for tax purposes) over the life of the property. The government dictates the life of the property for tax purposes. In general property is depreciated for tax purposes over the following periods:

- Land is not depreciated because it doesn't waste away
- Residential real estate is depreciated over 27½ years
- Commercial real estate is depreciated over 39 year
- Land improvements are depreciated over fifteen years
- Personal property is depreciated over various periods from three to seven years.

When you purchase real estate, take the time to identify the different types of property. If you don't the default method is to use the real estate assessors valuation of land and improvements. This is not accurate!

You can also go back and change the way you are depreciating property you purchased in the past!

The process of identifying the different types of property can be simple in the case of a single-family residence. Just identify the different types of property and get estimates of the replacement cost of each type of property.

Or, if the property is more complicated, you may need to hire engineers to do what is called a cost segregation analysis. This is more complicated and can be costly, but is frequently worth it because of the cost of larger multi-unit residential or commercial properties.

- **Advantage:**
  - Get quicker write-off for the purchase price of property.
- **How to implement**
  - Can be as simple as doing your own analysis of what was purchased and getting estimates of the replacement cost; or, for larger properties, get a professional cost segregation analysis;
  - Do an estimate of the potential benefits to see if the trouble is worth the effort.
- **Pitfalls**
  - Cost of a cost segregation analysis
  - Government may challenge, but they won't be successful of you document what was done.

Sell property that has a loss rather than trading it in

The like-kind exchange rules apply when business or rental property is traded-in for like kind property. Any gain or loss is not recognized, it is rolled into the replacement property. This is good in the case of property with a gain because it defers the gain until the replacement property is disposed of. However, this is not so good if the old property has a loss. It is generally best to recognize the loss as soon as possible because it may save taxes.

Instead of trading in business or rental property with a loss, sell it and recognize the loss immediately.

This may also be a good strategy if you have business or rental property with a gain if you have losses that can offset the gain.

Use a family limited partnership for estate planning and to shift income to family members in lower tax brackets

Transfer assets to a partnership with family members (commonly known as a family limited partnership) for estate planning purposes. In addition, you minimize tax on the family unit by shifting income to taxpayers in lower tax brackets. You keep management control over the property by being the general partner. Make yearly gifts to minimize or avoid gift tax.

- **Advantage:**
  - Lower tax on the family unit;
  - Achieve estate planning objectives.
- **How to implement**
  - Form a limited partnership;
  - Implement a plan to transfer interests in the partnership to family members;
  - Need appraisals of the property interests to determine the fair market value of property transferred.
- **Pitfalls**
  - Trouble and cost of maintaining the limited partnership;
  - Cost of appraisals of the property when you transfer interests;
  - Must have an motive other than mere tax avoidance.

Qualify as a real estate professional for tax breaks

Real estate professionals get favorable tax treatment. In order to qualify as a real estate professional, the tests for material participation discussed in the section on "Passive Activities" in chapter two (see page 14), you must meet two more tests:

- You spend at least 750 hours per year in "real property" trades or businesses in which you materially participate, and
- You spend more than one half of your working time on real estate activities in which you materially participate.

You can prove material participation by meeting some objective factors (i.e. working a certain number of yours) or subjective factors (i.e. provide "substantially all" management services). However, to meet the two additional tests to qualify as a real estate professional you must be able to prove with documentary evidence that you meet the tests. If you do not have the documentary evidence, the IRS can deny your status as a real estate professional.

- **Action Plan:**
  Keep a log or diary each year to prove that you meet these tests.

Create passive income to offset passive losses

Perhaps you have a business activity and can carve out some function performed in the activity and set-up another entity, say a partnership, to perform the function. If this is a passive activity for you, your income from the entity will be passive activity income that can be used to offset losses from passive activities.

- **Advantage:**
  - Use passive activity expenses and losses
- **How to implement**
  - Set-up another entity where you can be a passive investor (for instance a limited partnership where your spouse is the general partner and you are a limited partner) and it performs a function needed by another business which you own;
  - The other business pays the new entity for the

function which it previously did in house;
    - Need to demonstrate a non-tax motive for doing this. For instance estate planning or liability protection.

- **Pitfalls**
    - Cost of setting-up and operating another entity.

Chapter 8: Tax Strategies for Investments

Time the sale of assets to have offsetting gains and losses.

If you have property that you want to sell that has tax gains and losses, sell the property with losses in the same year that you sell property with gains. The losses will offset the gains. Losses can only be carried forward, not backward.

Transfer assets with gains to children to finance college

If you have children that are or will be going to college, consider transferring property with gains to them so they can sell the property and use the proceeds for their school expenses.

If they are in a lower tax bracket, the tax on the family unit will be lower.

- **Advantage:**
  - Lower overall tax to the family unit
- **How to implement**
  - Develop a structured plan of giving considering the gift and estate tax rules
- **Pitfalls**
  - Give up control of the assets

Buy your parents' home and rent it back to them

If your parent have lived in their home for several years, chances are it is paid-off and they are not able to itemize deductions.

Buy the property from them and rent it back to them. If they have owned and used the property as their principal residence for twenty four months out of the past five years they don't have pay tax on up to $250,000 of the gain if single, or up to $500,000 of the gain, if married.

You need to charge them fair-market rent, but landlords can reduce fair-market rent by twenty percent when renting to relatives because of the savings in maintenance and management costs (L.A. Bindseil, TC Memo 1983-411)

Appendices

Appendix A: Common Taxes

Here is a list of some common taxes:

1. Taxes on income.
2. Negative income tax—where people earning below a certain amount get money from the government.
3. Capital gains tax—lower taxes rates for gain from sale of property not used in a business, but the sale of some property used in a business also gets the lower tax rates.
4. Employment taxes; imposed by federal and state jurisdictions. Employers and employees pay these. Examples: social security taxes.
5. Self-employment taxes imposed on self-employed people when they are not subject to social security taxes as employees.
6. Property taxes assessed on the value of property
7. Inheritance tax
8. Estate and gift taxes; actually called transfer taxes because they are levied on the transfer of property. Guess what, there is a tax on giving something away! However most people don't run into it because of the $14,000 (in 2013 and 2014) exemption. The government doesn't want to get involved in collecting tax when Johnny gives a candy bar to Sue.
9. Sales taxes and use taxes; levied when something is sold or consumed. The use tax is comparable to the sales tax and comes into play when some buys something out of state and doesn't pay sales tax when the item is purchased.

10. Excise taxes based on the quantity, not the value of something purchased
11. Penalties: levies for failure not to do something. For instance there are penalties for failure to pay tax on time.
12. Fees are not considered taxes because they are levied as payment for a direct benefit to the individual paying.

Appendix B Income Tax Rate Schedules

Illustrative 2014 income tax rates on taxable income levels above the amount in the table and below the higher income level. The total income tax is the sum of the tax at each income level.

Rate	Single Filing Status	Joint Filing Status
10%	0	0
15%	9,076	18,151
25%	36,901	73,801
28%	89,351	148,851
33%	186,351	226,851
35%	405,101	405,101
39.6%	406,751	456,601

Appendix C: Medical Expense Reimbursement Plan

____ ("Employer") hereby establishes this Medical Expense Reimbursement Plan (the "Plan") for the exclusive benefit of its employees.

1. **Medical Expense Reimbursement**. Effective as of __________ _____, _____, Employer shall reimburse all eligible employees on a monthly basis for medical expenses included in Paragraph 3, below, that they incur on behalf of themselves, their spouses, and their dependents (as defined in Internal Revenue Code Section 152).
2. **Eligibility**. All employees shall be eligible except:
   - ❒ Those who work less than 35 hours per week.
   - ❒ Those who work less than nine months per year
   - ❒ Those under age 25
   - ❒ Those who have worked for employer for less than three years
3. **Qualifying Benefits**. "Medical expenses" shall include any expense qualifying under Internal Revenue Code Section 213(d).
4. **Maximum Benefits**. Employer shall limit reimbursement to any employee to ___________ per calendar year.
5. **Reimbursement**. Employer may reimburse employee for eligible expenses or pay medical providers directly. Employees applying for reimbursement shall submit all premium notices and eligible bills not more than 30 days after the end of the month in which they are paid. Failure to comply with this requirement may terminate employees' right to reimbursement for expenses not timely submitted.
6. **Unfunded Plan**. This plan shall be unfunded for purposes of the Employee Retirement Income Security Act (ERISA). Plan benefits shall be paid out of Employer's general assets.
7. **Coordination with Insurance**. Employer shall reimburse employee only in the event and to the extent that such expenses are not covered by any insurance policy, policies, or benefits, whether owned by Employer or employee, provided under any other accident or health insurance plan, or provided by federal or state governments or agencies.
8. **Amendment and Termination**. Employer reserves the right to amend or terminate the Plan at any time. Such action shall not deny any employee's right to claim reimbursement for expenses incurred before such amendment or termination. Employer shall give employees written notice of amendment or termination not more than 60 days before such termination.

9. **Notice**. Employer shall provide all eligible employees with a copy of this Plan within 90 days of eligibility.
10. **Exclusions**. Employer intends that this Plan and all benefits payable under this Plan shall qualify for exclusion from eligible employees' gross income under Internal Revenue Code Sections 105 and 106. Employer reserves the right to amend or terminate this Plan in the event that such benefits no longer qualify for such exclusion.

In witness whereof, Employer adopts this plan on ______________________ ______, ___________.

________________ __________________________________Signature

"A taxpayer is someone who works for the federal government but doesn't have to take a civil-service exam."

Ronald Reagan

"No man's life, liberty, or property is safe while Congress is in session."

Mark Twain

Appendix D: Reasonable Compensation for a Shareholder Employee of an S Corporation

What are the IRS guidelines for determining Reasonable Compensation for a shareholder-employee of an S Corp?

The instructions to the Form 1120S, U.S. Income Tax Return for an S Corporation, state: "Distributions and other payments by an S corporation to a corporate officer must be treated as wages to the extent the amounts are reasonable compensation for services rendered to the corporation."

The key to establishing reasonable compensation is determining what the shareholder-employee did for the S corporation. In addition to the shareholder-employee direct generation of gross receipts, the shareholder-employee should also be compensated for administrative work performed.

There are no specific guidelines for reasonable compensation in the Code or the Regulations. The various courts that have ruled on this issue based their determinations on the facts and circumstances of each case.

Some factors considered by the courts in determining reasonable compensation:

- Training and experience
- Duties and responsibilities
- Time and effort devoted to the business
- What comparable businesses pay for similar services
- The use of a formula to determine compensation
- Payments to non-shareholder employees
- Dividend history
- Timing and manner of paying bonuses to key people
- Compensation agreements

Appendix E:
Business Entities Related to Goals

Your Goal:	**Start a Business**	**Hold Assets**	**Earn Income**	**Offer Benefits *or* Split Income**
Tax Treatment:	**Sole Proprietorship**	**Partnership**	**S-Corporation**	**C-Corporation**
State Filing:	None	Articles of Organization	Articles of Organization or Incorporation	Articles of Organization or Incorporation
Tax Filing:	Schedule C	File Form 1065; use Schedule K1 to report pass-through income to partners or members	File Form 1120S; use Schedule K1 to report pass-through income to shareholders	File Form 1120 or 1120-A and pay tax on net income at corporate rates
Employment Tax:	Net income subject to self-employment tax	Ordinary income generally subject to self-employment tax; passive income is not	Must pay "reasonable salary" subject to FICA; pass-through income not subject to employment tax	Salary income subject to FICA; dividends not subject to employment tax
Employee Benefits:	Limited (proprietor is "self employed")	Limited (partners/members are "self-employed")	Limited (>2% shareholders and spouses are "self-employed")	Greatest variety of deductible programs
Personal Liability:	Proprietor personally liable for business. Consider organizing single-member LLC to limit personal liability.	General partners personally liable for business. Most advisors recommend organizing LLC or LLP to limit personal liability.	Shareholders not personally liable for business. State law may favor organizing LLC or LLP to be taxed as S-corp.	Shareholders not personally liable for business. State law may favor organizing LLC or LLP to be taxed as C-corp.

***Your Goal*:**	**Start a Business**	**Hold Assets**	**Earn Income**	**Offer Benefits** *or* **Split Income**
Tax Treatment:	**Sole Proprietorship**	**Partnership**	**S-Corporation**	**C-Corporation**
Other:	Consider hiring family to establish deductible benefit programs Consider forming S-corp as income grows	Generally best vehicle for generating passive income from rents, royalties, etc.	Ownership limits apply (<101 shareholders; all must be US taxpayers)	Corporation can "zero out" income to avoid corporate tax or retain income to be taxed at lower corporate rate Beware special rules for personal service corporations & personal holding companies

Appendix F:
Retirement Plans for Small Business Employers

	SEP-IRA	SIMPLE IRA and SIMPLE § 401(k)	Qualified Plan
Contri-bution Deadline	Due date of employer's tax return (including extensions).	Salary deferral contributions to SIMPLE IRAs must be made within 30 days after the end of the month for which the contributions are to be made. Matching or nonelective contributions are due on the due date of the employer's tax return (including extensions). Salary deferral contributions to SIMPLE § 401(k)s follow the qualified plan rule.	Salary deferrals must be deposited as soon as they can be segregated from the employer's assets, but no later than the 15th day of the month following the month received. Employer contributions are due on the due date of the employer's tax return (including extensions). **Note:** For a defined benefit plan subject to minimum funding requirements, contributions are due in quarterly installments (April 15, July 15, October 15, and January 15 of the following year).
Contri-bution Limit	Lesser of \$52,000 for 2014 or 25%[1] of participant's compensation.[2] Participants age 50 and older can	**Employee:** Salary reduction contributions up to \$17,500 for 2014. Participants age 50 and older can make catch-up	**Defined Contribution Plans:** *Money Purchase:* Lesser of \$52,000 for 2014 or 100%[1] of participant's compensation.[2]

	SEP-IRA	SIMPLE IRA and SIMPLE § 401(k)	Qualified Plan
	make catch-up contributions of $5,500.	contributions of $5,500 **Employer contributions:** *Either* dollar-for-dollar matching contributions, up to 3% of employee's compensation,[3] *or* fixed nonelective contributions of 2% of compensation.[2]	*Profit Sharing:* Lesser of $52,000 for 2014 or 100%[1] of participant's compensation.[2] *401(k):* Employee elective deferrals of $17,500 for 2014.[4] Participants age 50 and older can make catch-up contributions of $5,500 for 2014. **Defined Benefit Plans:** Limit on annual benefit is no greater than the lesser of $210,000 for 2014 or 100% of the participant's average compensation for his or her highest 3 consecutive calendar years.
Deduction Limit	25%[1] of all participants' compensation.	Same as maximum contribution.	**Defined Contribution Plans:** *Money Purchase:* 25%[1] of all participants' compensation.[2] *Profit-Sharing:* 25%[1] of all participants' compensation.[2] **Defined Benefit Plans:** Based on actuarial

	SEP-IRA	SIMPLE IRA and SIMPLE § 401(k)	Qualified Plan
			assumptions and computations. Combined deduction limit for defined benefit and defined contribution plan is greater of 25% of all participants' compensation or amount necessary to meet minimum funding standards of defined benefit plans.
Deadline to Set Up Plan	Due date of employer's tax return (including extensions). May use Form 5305-SEP.	Any date from January 1 through October 1 of the calendar year. For a new employer that comes into existence after October 1, as soon as administratively feasible. May use Forms 5304-SIMPLE or 5305-SIMPLE.	By the end of the tax year. Must adopt written plan document: IRS-approved master or prototype plan or individually designed plan.
Salary Deferrals	Not permitted.	Allowed up to contribution limit, above.	**Defined Contribution Plans:** Allowed up to contribution limit, above. **Defined Benefit Plan:** Not permitted.
Nondis-crimination Testing	Not applicable.	Not applicable to SIMPLE IRAs. SIMPLE § 401(k)s are deemed to satisfy	**Defined Contribution Plans:** Employee elective deferrals or contributions, and

	SEP-IRA	SIMPLE IRA and SIMPLE § 401(k)	Qualified Plan
		nondiscrimination requirements.	employer matches or nonelective contributions, must be limited for the group of highly compensated employees based on the averages for the non-highly compensated employees, unless the plan is designed as a safe harbor plan or has a compliant automatic enrollment feature. **Defined Benefit Plan:** Must demonstrate that it does not discriminate in favor of highly compensated employees by satisfying general test (i.e., each rate group under the plan satisfies § 410(b) as though it were a separate plan) or adopting a design-based safe harbor.
Form 5500 Filing	Not required if employer furnishes employee with a copy of the completed and unmodified Form 5305-SEP used to create the SEP, and notifies each SEP	Not required for SIMPLE IRAs. Required for SIMPLE § 401(k)s.	Required.

	SEP-IRA	SIMPLE IRA and SIMPLE § 401(k)	Qualified Plan
	participant in writing of any employer contributions made under the contribution agreement to the participant's IRA each year. DOL Regs. § 2520.104-48.		
Employer Eligibility	Any employer.	Employers that had no more than 100 employees who earned at least $5,000 in the previous year.	Any employer.
Employee Eligibility	Must include all employees who (1) are at least 21 years old, (2) who have been employed for 3 of the 5 preceding years, and (3) who earn at least $550 in 2013 (same in 2012 and 2011). This amount is subject to adjustment for inflation.	SIMPLE IRAs must include employees who earned at least $5,000 in any 2 preceding calendar years and who are reasonably expected to earn $5,000 in the current year. SIMPLE § 401(k)s follow the rule for qualified plans.	Must include employees who are at least 21 years old and who have performed at least 1 year of service.

[1] Net earnings from self-employment must take the contribution into account.
[2] Compensation generally is limited to $260,000 for 2014
[3] Under a SIMPLE § 401(k) plan, compensation generally is limited to $260,000 for 2014.
[4] A § 401(k) plan must be included in a money purchase or profit-sharing plan and the combined employer contributions and elective deferrals are limited to the lesser of $52,000 for 2014 or 1005 of participant's compensation.

"I owe the government $3,400 in taxes.
So I sent them two hammers and a toilet seat."

Michael McShane

Appendix G: Individual Retirement Plans for Individuals

Type of Plan	Contribution Deadline	Contribution Limit	Deduction Limit	Deadline to Set Up Plan
Traditional IRA[1]	Due date for filing individual's tax return (not including extensions). **Note:** Contributions cannot be made in year in which individual reaches age $70^1/_2$ or later.	Lesser of $5,500 for 2014 and 2013 ($5,000 for 2012) or individual's compensation.[2] Participants age 50 and older can make catch-up contribution of $1,000 (not indexed for inflation). *Spousal IRA:* If individual files joint return and has less compensation than his or her spouse, contribution is limited to lesser of $5,500 for 2014 and 2013 ($5,000 for 2012) plus age 50 catch-up contribution, or total compensation of both spouses reduced by spouse's IRA contributions (traditional and Roth). Total combined contributions for married couple can be $11,000 for 2014 and 2013 ($10,000 for 2012) plus age 50 catch-up contribution.	Same as maximum contribution, subject to phase-out rules.[3] *Spousal IRA:* If married couple with unequal compensation file joint return, deduction limit of spouse with less compensation is limited to lesser of $5,500 for 2014 and 2013 ($5000 for 2012) plus age 50 catch-up contribution, or total compensation of both spouses, reduced by contribution by spouse with greater taxable compensation to traditional and Roth IRAs.	Due date for filing individual's tax return (not including extensions) so long as not age $70^1/_2$ by end of the year. If married, both spouses may set up IRA, but cannot participate in the same IRA. May use Forms 5305 and 5305-A.
Roth IRA[1]	Due date for filing individual's tax return (not including extensions).	Lesser of $5,500 for 2014 ($5,500 for 2013 and $5,000 for 2012) or individual's compensation.[2] Participants age 50 and older can make catch-up contribution of	Contributions not deductible.	Due date for filing individual's tax return (not including extensions). May use Forms 5305-

Type of Plan	Contribution Deadline	Contribution Limit	Deduction Limit	Deadline to Set Up Plan
		$1,000 (not indexed for inflation). The maximum contribution limit is subject to phase-out rules.[4]		R, 5305-RA and 5305-RB.

[1] This IRA is another tax-deferred savings instrument used for retirement by an individual in addition to an employer-provided retirement plan. Beginning in 2010, restrictions on Roth IRA conversions, based on adjusted gross income and filing status, no longer apply. For a discussion of Roth IRA conversions, see X, J.

[2] Compensation for this purpose is earned income, which includes earnings from self-employment.

[3] For 2014, if you are covered by your employer's retirement plan, the phase-out rules reduce the deduction amount if your modified adjusted gross income (AGI) is between $96,000 and $116,000 ($95,000 and $115,000 for 2013, $92,000 and $112,000 for 2012) for a married couple filing a joint return or a qualifying widow(er); between $60,000 and $70,000 ($59,000 and $69,000 for 2013, $58,000 and $68,000 for 2012) for a single individual or head of household; or less than $10,000 for a married individual filing a separate return. For 2014, if you are married and *not* covered by your employer's retirement plan but your spouse *is* covered by an employer plan, your deduction is phased out if your modified AGI is between $181,000 and $191,000 ($178,000 and $188,000 for 2013, $173,000 and $183,000 for 2012) for a married couple filing jointly; or less than $10,000 for a married couple filing separately (if you did not live with your spouse at any time during the year, you get the full deduction). *See* § 219(g).

[4] For 2014, the phase-out rules reduce the maximum contribution that can be made by an individual with a modified AGI between $181,000 to $191,000 ($178,000 and $188,000 for 2013, $173,000 and $183,000 for 2012) if married filing jointly; for a single individual, head of household or married filing separately who did not live with the spouse at any time during the year, between $114,000 and $129,000 ($112,000 and $127,000 for 2013, $110,000 and $125,000 for 2012); and between $0 and $10,000 for married filing separately and who lived with the spouse during the year. *See* § 408A(c)(3)(B)(ii), as redesignated by P.L. 109-222, § 512(a), effective for taxable years beginning after Dec. 31, 2009.

Appendix H:
What Qualifies as a Home Office

To qualify as a Home Office the use of the home must fall into one of the following two categories:

1. Business use must be regularly and exclusive
    a. as the principal place of business
        i. A home office will qualify as a principal place of business where it is a place of business used by the taxpayer for the administrative or management activities of any trade or business of the taxpayer if there is no other fixed location of the trade or business where the taxpayer conducts substantial administrative or management activities of the trade or business. Examples of administrative or managerial activities are billing customers, clients, or patients; keeping books and records; ordering supplies; setting up appointments; and forwarding orders or writing reports. A home office will not be disqualified for any of the following reasons:
            1. Others conduct administrative or management activities at other locations
            2. □The taxpayer conducts administrative or management activities at places that are not fixed locations of the business, such as in a car or a hotel room
            3. The taxpayer occasionally conducts minimal administrative or management activities at a fixed location outside the home

            4. □The taxpayer conducts substantial non-administrative or non-managerial activities at a fixed location outside the home or
            5. □The taxpayer has suitable space to conduct administrative or managerial activities outside the home, but chooses to use the home office for those activities.
        ii. As a place of business which is used by patients, clients, or customers in meeting or dealing with the taxpayer in the normal course of the taxpayer's trade or business

2. In the case of a separate structure which is not attached to the dwelling unit in connection with the taxpayer's business
    a. Business uses that must be regular but not necessarily exclusive
        i. As a storage unit for the inventory or, product samples of the taxpayer: or
        ii. In the taxpayer's trade or business of providing day care services for children

Appendix I:
How to Deduct Home Office Used by Your Corporation

A taxpayer cannot deduct expenses attributable to a home office rented by the taxpayer to his employer (the corporation) during any period in which the taxpayer uses the home office in performing services as an employee of the employer (the corporation). Internal Revenue Code Section 280A(c)6)

How to deduct home office expenses:

An employer can deduct business expenses reimbursed to an employee through a Accountable Expense Reimbursement Plan.

In the case of the home office, the employee figures the business expenses used for the home office and submits an expenses report to the employer which the employer pays for through an accountable expense reimbursement plan.

The home office expenses are the ratable portion of the common expenses such as interest, property taxes, utilities, maintenance, etc. plus the direct expenses (e.g. those expenses directly related to the home office portion of the dwelling). Figure the ratable portion by dividing the square footage of the home office by the total square footage of the dwelling unit.

I suggest that the taxpayer get reimbursed on a regular basis, such as monthly, quarterly, or semi-annual.

Index

L

M

N

O

P

R

S

T

W

Acknowledgments

I would like to thank my friend and colleague Wayne A. McFadden, Esq. who I have had the pleasure of working with over the past twenty years. I have benefited enormously from his wisdom and experience, from the experience of working with many mutual clients going through the legal process, and with the opportunity to go before the United States Tax Court and various administrative appeals. He manifests the power of faith!

I would also like to thank my friends in the Certified Tax Coach Community and, in particular, the following individuals associated with Certified Tax Coach and Tax Coach Software. They had the foresight to create a vehicle to communicate and deliver the value of *ProActive* tax planning.

- Dominique Molina, CPA, CTC; founder of Certified Tax Coach
- Edward Lyon, Esq., Co-founder of Tax Coach Software, "The funniest tax guy in the nation"
- Keith VandeStadt, Co-founder of Tax Coach Software

Rupert Hart, creative genius and author, whom I first met in a Toastmasters Club. He has cajoled and inspired me to bring this book to completion. Rupert, thank you!

About the author

Frederick A. Thompson, CPA, CTC is the founder and principal of Frederick A. Thompson, CPA an Accountancy Corporation. He lives in Redwood City California with his wife. He has four grown daughters. With his wife, Lydia, Fred enjoys hiking the mountain trails in Northern California, walking the beach, as well as reading and travelling. He believes that balance and sharing with others are the keys to happiness.

Fred concentrates on *ProActive* tax planning and is also a Certified Tax Coach. He specializes in helping his clients reduce their taxes to the absolute legal minimum and protecting them from tax audits.

He focuses his extensive experience on working with real estate professionals and investors. Fred has worked with real estate developers, building operators, brokers, and agents. In addition, he is an affiliate member of his local real estate association. Fred is a frequent speaker to real estate groups about tax reduction strategies. He has testified in federal and California courts on family law matters and business disputes.

Fred received his CPA certificate from California in 1974. To qualify he had to take college courses in business law, accounting, auditing, and taxation. And in addition pass a rigorous 2½ day board examination administered by the State of California. Each year since then he has taken continuing education courses in business and taxation to keep up with the ever-changing laws and regulations. Every two years the State of California requires him to take eighty hours of continuing education courses.

He is known for helping individuals and businesses understand and navigate the complex financial, business and tax world. He believes in empowering individuals to take control of their future.

Fred's office is in San Mateo, California. He can be reached at (650) 343-5965 or by e-mail fred@fthompsoncpa.com

Made in the USA
Monee, IL
08 November 2026

68085576R00066